BOOK OF INTERLUDES

GRACE SHUYI LIEW

© 2016 Grace Shuyi Liew
First edition 2016. Printed in the USA by Bookmobile.

ISBN: 978-1-939781-30-7

Designed & cover letterpress printed by Erica Mena
on paper from Burning Deck.

This book is available as an ebook from Anomalous Press.
www.anomalouspress.org/books/interludes.php

DISLOYAL

You dream of blonde women (not ponytail-blonde) (just cropped blonde) whose husky bodies barricade your way. It's not them you want (it's them) (it's not). They look at you (unslanted) (full frontal). These days it's passé to fuck people you disdain. Disembodied despair is a myth. It's a scentless dream so your fingers exit her legs unsoured (a narrative flaw) (never having been). The stories tight and pined for like wet grass (all lies) give you encouragement. To your lidded eyes the whole piece of sky is real.

The year of light winds brought love and wellness (in opposition) and five kinds of color (grief). In a tug you release red (not liquid) (just like that). Bare brown nights are for moving away from a perfect sky (small stink of a shared mattress). On a bus that takes you only to the middle you throw your hands against her midnight lap (survive) (survive) and remember a memory you do not have: your grandmother pulling up grey roots of groundnut in between lean trees. A fingertip indents a saucer-sized nipple.

You wait while she waits for her self-portrait to dry. For this occasion you bought her a mirror (full-length) (black-gilded). She is sitting. The canvas tilts and you are locked. A bit of darkness is reproduced (in watercolor). The white of time lodged in your throat (drying fast). Her squiggly lines, your throat. Her dripping paint, your throat. Her slow turns, her coin-sized blood, her human mouth. What it means to keep away (pre-time)? Hear grace? You rejoin the buttons on her shirt (this return precedes arousal).

So much leans on an original (the first) (the pre-). So much requires a past (the line in the sand). Your self-perception cannot bear the smallness of your first memories. First boy (the one with the soft body) (always they will be soft). First girl (punching your own slack belly). You're the dog that will leap into any open car door (yes!) (no) (stupid isn't this) (instinct isn't this) (the shortcoming of an imagination), a dirty city street tonguing paper scraps (discarded announcements) (other people's love notes). None more ethereal than you in a hand-me-down body (willingness to be stretched).

You walk down a dust path to encounter warm happy days (straighten out your postcolonial tan lines). How quickly you wear through city after city, the lack of light strange and silent (pasty white men presuming they are the only one "capable of" discerning the palpable present) (all its concomitant "beautiful complications") (decidedly of "our times"). Still (!) for the Holidays this year you are bringing one of them home again (again) (You have long known the best ways to disclose yourself in a moment of panic): (Can't stop) longing for a sun that desiccates rather than animates.

INTERLUDE, DISLOYAL

Mark your presence out in the wild, face up, physically open,

alongside perilous dips and cracks in the weather,
familiar expressions emerging from rock faces cut from moonlight.

    A moonlight trained to stretch and trap those footfalls approaching exposure.

The edges will always be colored.

In this natural phenomena: Specter of a half girl, small beaming, splashing in a green lake, dark hair cropped at mid-cheek, her memory of her mother scant.

    Inside you is a mother wounded from the death of her mother.

    Inside her is a mother who never recovered from the birth of her children.

See how water parts for her.

DISLOYAL

You are gonna be okay you say (closed in by bodies) (imaginary pangs) as you familiarize yourself with the facts of your dislocation. You were never a girl: your grimy denouncements have always been (mis-)taken as unhinged (orbits of a soft mind). Not that you didn't earnestly imagine pleasure at every chance (fumbling at your own body) (an avatar made swollen by a selfish appetite) (pliant tongue lapping through a chest opening). You lie spread eagle and through your teeth to pacify (/investigate) movements that reverberate. (Awaiting the day all your fingers end up inside yourself.)

You allow (expect) consensual captivity of your body to bring you refuge the way every sick form of universal truth erects a savage (original parts of a whole) in order to imagine freedom. Sex between ciswomen is mirrored geography (or out-of-date adage) (?) Bending at the waist (either backward or forward) is still an imprecision so ingrained it can only evoke bondage (take it) or charity (asking for it). Neither satisfies a Syaitan spinning yarn. When permission (accruing power) collides with objectification (receding humanity) a nag in your heart calls softly to the rainfall of another country.

Melancholia in the body falls in love by flaunting its aptitude at mimicking grace (or lightness) (arduous passes) (lit/vanished lit/vanished) No one taught you (yet you know) how to preserve a love at the cost of your own vanishing (palms that leak/scoops of light) how your role is always to await spoilage (hushed under double-triple-thighs/yanked from a hiding place/pacified to the tune of a white pulse) Let me see, let me see: how mimicry nurses melancholy/how your every ratap-rintihan attunes to stillness (shhh).

To ask for likeness in exchange for lightheartedness is a necessary (unnecessary) cruelty. You've been there before: paper planes that won't fold themselves (unthinkable to defy a birthright) (to rise out of flatness), a face that parades singularity. You would really love to keep living on flesh. You would really love to forget the past (straighten out those bends in your yester-limbs). The people you have _____ all line up to ring your doorbell with questions; their decoys walk right through the walls of your home.

INTERLUDE, PROCESSES

I sit on a bench
Next to a river
Consumed by the urge to
Wet myself. I could just do it
Now, sitting. I could loosen up
A trickle, roll my body
Across the river brink like a
Carpet gathering itself. I try
To hold in memory
The feelings I'm in danger of
Losing. Days like this
The human condition is
Beating the shit out of me.
By shit I mean men
Crawling out of my ear
Holes who all start out
White except for their eyes that
Narrow into lightless
Slits, stab and stab and
Stab me before fading
Back into unbounded space,
Their dead god's right.

The right to occupy a body,
Any body,
Gives itself to no one
Else. My
Cunt meanwhile gulps like a
Blowfish, bloat salted with
Pretend poison,
Stabilized by anal fins, a
Low pressure in the rump.
Today the river is
Frothy after a rain.
I envision myself thirsting
before sleep.
Nothing that comes out of
Me is an accident.
After the fact,
The gathering:
The violences we are most
familiar with remain untold.

INTERLUDE, DISLOCATED

For the fact that never again will you encounter an entire city of people hushed to a fault. For the fact that the pulse low on your spine is already hardening, small hollow earth, a round bowl with no opening despite its need. For the fact that night heat, posturing lightness, rises inside you like an airlift. For the fact that you are already someone else looking back in time. For the fact that you filed down your sharp edges in order to carry your mother's worry. For the fact that alienation is not a supplication you outgrow. But the fact isn't that anguish must be passed down through generations, or even that bodies accumulate peril by nature—must every name matched to a face matched to a body matched to a life matched to a death be matched to a red string looped around an entire continent? When power cultivates its own logic, how do forking paths afford wanderers? Poetry isn't located in aftermaths. The ties that bind are all banal. Watch out for tongues that carry virtuous song crying fate. Dare you find mercy in a bitterness swelling to choke all exit doors.

INTERLUDE, METALLIC

I have never
found a sustainable container for my own words.

The resounding dissatisfaction—tonight
I hated the purchase of a body

I tiptoed into bed before my ilk
sterilized the air

Without consent my strides are collected.
A metaphor endures hollow dangers.

There was a time I couldn't stop myself
from anything and then

I could. I don't reverse engineer
the stains on my white sheets for myself

To un-see, to pre-see, to march
latent cognition into

an unmarked grave
Something too tidy here, this kind of

soundlessness that cuts.

INTERLUDE, BERLIN: AN ESSAY

Arrangement is luck. I wake up one morning to a swollen top lip. Each day I stare in the mirror at a face formed and reformed by disparity. Probably a combination of bad sleep, lack of fruit in my diet, and inertia. Or an infection of a two-month-old philtrum piercing.

Berliners apologize to me, a voyeur, for the gray December skies. We are three days away from the longest night of the year. By 4pm it's pitch dark. The right conditions can split wide open what's self-evident. My top lip, puffy as a baby's red-tinged cheek, marks me as transitory, and I am free to appear safe to others. Embedded under that lip is an assurance of evaporation. The white pus is wet and persistent.

Google tells me to check for heat at the affected site. Saltwater or another kind of purge. I order milchkaffees at cafes and flirt with women and forget to check for pain or redness. I become newly private as the proprietor of diminishing smiles.

An ex emails me about under-bridge parties with marginalia reminders of the ways this city gestures at despair that amount to universal hospitality. If I am a girl dispersing into invisible mental fragments, then I didn't attend the bridge party, didn't kiss a perfect-skinned German girl.

In spite of my disappearing face, in spite of my swollen top lip, I let my white-loving splinter bury itself further under my skin.

I angle for perfect eyebrows. White women wish me a happy morning that day I slept only three hours. On the U-Bahn my eyes well up. Observation originated from cities, and I only want to listen. To see is to approximate the source of lack, and teary eyes become fully functional to recreate perception.

In another way I have been displaced before the time of the city.

I used to travel well. Now I wear my body as infiltration. The exchange of spaces occupies me up to the last unvetted thought. People unwilling to remain in sadness wear their bodies as readily charged, ready to flex violence against the other bodies entering their spheres.

I cross when it's red and yell in Chinese at a car screeching to a halt. I know how language flattens lives, but not knowing German aerates me into dimensions. Xenophobia can't reach me via sound.

I make myself enter every one of them even though the English bookstores haunt me. The roof of the building is misshapen under the white weight of expatriates hungry for the Beats, the Lost Generation, the Brat Pack. Exile does not discriminate privacy. I add some color and gender variance to the window displays to recentralize exclusion. The feminine mystique takes pride in chewing with sealed lips.

A British-accented owner asks about my lip, directs a customer toward Bret

Easton Ellis.

I sneak a book of poetry under my parka into the hail and rain.

A market crowds the Berlin wall. What do you see when you see me, I want to grab a person by the elbow and back them into a wall.

Anger can froth some mobility into sadness, even if not all sadness is static. With some lag I group all my fears into a tall white wall I forget about and repeatedly knock into. The spiders in a dream scuttle toward the wall and scale it with ease.

A New Yorker critic of Berlin's Memorial to the Murdered Jews of Europe invites his reader to envision this: Germany affecting sincerity through individual citizens, each carving one of six million names onto the cement blocks. When I visit at night the children are still skipping in penitence. Why should it have been left unmarked? Why prize the pristine gray of a blank slate over candor?

There is a naiveté in isolation. What does it mean to share a birth country? *Your fingers curl outward instead of inward.* This is how my mother valorizes with guilt my unflinching strut exiting the familial circle.

I have no desire to infantilize the trope of the mother. Here are my movements flinted with forgottenness, disallowed any intervention. I become attached to the swell in my lip. On the last day I did fix my gaze on a stranger: *Tell me about the last time you were unhappy with me.*

INTERLUDE: FOR BODIES, PASSING SLOWLY IN THE NIGHT

Out of the last livable ship, onto
        a raft,
        overboard.

To toe the line of punishment meted out by an arm bloated
        with death, severed at the shoulder

You are forced to stare.
        Liminal or livable, liminal or livable.

This isn't a corpse-arm you know, this lily-blue and grotesque,
        this voided will, this whitened finger that

points,

asking for ways forward or ways to be done for:

        It was only a week ago that you'd thought you were dead?

Your eyesight whimpers, unmoved by
        the last inhabitable place on earth.

The pain in your shell the pain

        of unreachable tracts, of having been left, of fixture
        into a landmark, passable,

but permanent,

passable, but

permanent.

You write everything down, write it until it no longer wants to be

written, until the suture lines

expose themselves like raw belly like sureness

When the chance to

leave everything untouched surges through you like new life,

is it still you? You?

So few?

INTERLUDE: TEACH YOUR TONGUE NEW SOUNDS

In this formation the snow is
jagged, even though by nature

cold water breaks shapes. Just how
natural laws turn aberrant sometimes,

gale-mother chancing lone, paled by
commotion and its din of signified

worth. I want to ruin your life
it's said. So the frost in its black

wet might want to numb
a revolution. Else why else

come up from under the covers,
as if love would move beyond

displeasing for just anyone – – – – No
no – no – ! Abide! – No – Even the gloom

in a puddle has origins in ease, so
then I will still eat from your palm

in the dark. I will still aberrate
like a good girl, just beneath

your hoodwinking breaths/breasts.
Somehow mothering in this climate

feels opulent. Or it's just
spilled ice making myself up

as dislocated, two/three spheres of
bodies spat out of a lack of friction,

such readinesses so
interminable I hunger

to gather for return
all the names you have given me.

INTERLUDE, NEW YORK: AN ESSAY

The bus pulls into Chinatown before anyone has risen. Rows of shop shutters tremble behind the freezing white mist. The cold slaps you into place. In less than a day the year will turn over and burn.

Duality applies here: most alone, most accompanied. Most enclosed, most vast. Most filthy, most pure.

Closest to death, closest to not yet dying.

Your small, bright orange suitcase barely fits under the metal turnstile. You climb onto a train and rattle toward your next destination.

You come up on the sidewalk dotted with black stains—skeptical but not idle, not contradicted in equal weight against what is sought. Nothing but to begin doubting. Emerging is one of your favorite things to do.

You could walk up and out of a subway station forever.

In this language the words to signify the people dear to you are too singular. You are here to see old friends. By the time you have lined up the correct metaphors to approximate the layers of how you feel the feeling's already become something entirely else.

Again you slip back into refusing to recognize faces.

At the New Year's Eve party you are too busy mapping the contours of time to stall with small talk. To assimilate is to have regressed past the point of inhuman.

By the moment of drunken hunger, past midnight, kissed twice, you are incoherent and sobbing: I am not one of you. I speak all the ways you ask of me but I am not one of you.

What you have stolen I don't even want anymore.

To frame noise as extraneous to knowledge is to be stuck in the process of awakening. Perpetually regaining self-consciousness. The slightest siren, thinnest rubbish truck beep, faintest titter around street corners, barely discernible.

But why should it have been you to cry?

Where you are staying the bathtub doesn't drain. Your underfeet stick to the grime and make no offers of resistance.

What triggers the contagion of decay is not its desire to fall away but its insistence on renouncing rapture. Now, no one can delight. No one sings. There are only scraps of paper rubbish scissoring air. Days later we fall out of bed. Nothing changes in the morning.

On the last day of your visit you take a train to the airport but arrive in a taxicab. Your eyes, hollowed from the journey, knock over the bartender's. She sends you a stiff drink for free then keeps her back to you until you finish and climb off the barstool.

All the planes are on time.

INTERLUDE, PUBLICS: AN ESSAY

I wanted melancholy to claim some potential, so at the sight of fresh-cut grass today I implored my sense-receptors to digress beyond their usual threshold.

Together they deliberated.

Wear a coat, I was told, and keep it on everywhere you go. Make a show of showing up to make an appearance, perpetually ricocheted by conflicting engagements.

Make a ghost of your poise.

Others always will want to know if you speak Asian languages you don't speak, hitch you to a framework, aerate you into sufferer.

A circle looped inside another bigger circle is predetermined to forage ceaselessly for warmth to mistake it for recognition.

I take walks alone now.

Without dogs on leashes or a palm to advise bruises, solitude under an open afternoon sky lashes at me like a shadow ripped.

Mirroring to find yourself is to invisibilize yourselves.

When an orb containing our cumulated doldrums is excavated, who can claim rights to it?

An entire subcontinent kneeled before the execution before the sky turned over and vanished us.

Placidity idled like a digging hoe meanwhile.

INTERLUDE, ON BORROWED LAND

That season you declared in delicate ways your inclination to eat
everything within reach, snap-closing a coin purse to find usefulness
already dispensed. This flatscape, coniferous. The first winter
of slack winds, the wilderness, badlands, tracking you back through
doors you'd long ago torn off, entryways still adorned with lovely
hinges, a bare surroundings whiter than teeth. Slowly your steel face
poised to trickle, unbroken the way of water, until the long day
aimed its arrow south of you. You could have worried more
given the facts of your life. When observing struggle a heart
distends in order to learn fear. An uplift is bitterness homebound.

INTERLUDE, FINAL LYRIC

Come though, come. On the heaviest day of snow please
lock and flog me up. The last time I cried I was reading the news
about a death: A girl broke her foot on a hike so
        a boy went for help.

Not because the boy got lost and died, not because I keep
paying with another sharp stripe to my back—Every day a
girl turns to find him gone, even now they
        can't part with this fear.

Do you: Carry murder in yourself? Travel back when you push me
against a wall? Find a small perfect match in me? The smoke you
blow my way stays a cloud in time, conceal-containing all the misled
        distances we kept,

until a line finally snaps, a line whose last bird has flown, how it's the
slightest smile that derides, slightest wind that carries my
song, incantation of *hit me hit me hit me*, though you never did,
        no you never would.

ACKNOWLEDGMENTS

Thank you to the editors of *alice blue review*, *Juked*, *The Rusty Toque*, and *Matrix* for first publishing several of the poems collected in this chapbook.

Thank you to Vancouver Poetry House for featuring sections of "Disloyal" as one of their *Ten Best Poems of 2015*.

Many of these poems came out of moments of intense unsettling (usually interrupted by intense desire). I am grateful to Krystle Wong for our lifelong conversations that shaped some of the emotions presented in this book. Thank you too for the weeks of refuge in Berlin.

I couldn't have gotten by without the urgent talks with Ginger Ko and Melanie McCuin. Thank you for mentorship and kindnesses from Sanjam Ahluwalia, Ann Cummins, Arianne Burford, Justin Bigos, Erin Stalcup, and all who kept me attentive in Flagstaff. Thank you to the Watering Hole community and teachers for modeling what's possible. Thanks too to my family, for what's unsaid, and to Berk, for all the love and latitude.

The sixteenth book in the Anomalous Press chapbook series, this book was designed and the cover letterpress printed by Erica Mena on paper from Burning Deck in a limited edition of 100 copies.

Anomalous Press is dedicated to the diffusion of writing in the forms it can take. We're searching for imaginary solutions in this exceptional universe. We're thinking about you and that thing you wrote one time and how you showed it to us and we blushed.

www.anomalouspress.org

 **Grace Shuyi Liew is** the author of *Prop* (winner of Ahsahta Press's 2015 Chapbook Prize). Her poetry can also be found in *West Branch, cream city review, Bone Bouquet, Twelfth House, H_ngm_n, PANK*, and others. She is a contributing editor for *Waxwing* and editor for *Anthropoid*. She has won awards to attend Squaw Valley Writers Workshop, Aspen Summer Words, and others. She is from Malaysia and currently resides in Louisiana, whose air is wet hot like home.

Available from **Anomalous Press**:

1. *Courting an Orbit* by Alma Baumwoll

2. *An Introduction to Venantius Fortunatus for Schoolchildren or Understanding the Medieval Concept World through Metonymy* by Mike Schorsch

3. *The Continuing Adventures of Alice Spider* by Janis Freegard

4. *Ghost* by Sarah Tourjee

5. *Mystérieuse* by Éric Suchère, translated by Sandra Doller
selected by Christian Hawkey

6. *The Everyday Maths* by Liat Berdugo
selected by Cole Swensen

7. *Smedley's Secret Guide to World Literature by Jonathan Levy Wainwright, IV, age 15* by Askold Melnyczuk

8. *His Days Go By The Way Her Years*
by Ye Mimi, translated by Steve Bradbury

9. *Mimi and Xavier Star In A Museum That Fits Entirely In One's Pocket* by Becca Barniskis

10. *Outer Pradesh* by Nathaniel Mackey

11. *The Occitan Goliard Songs of Clamanc Llansana followed by a French prose poem of Marcel de l'Aveugle* translated and introduced by Kit Schluter

12. *Third Person Singular* by Rosmarie Waldrop

13. *Anatomy of a Museum* by A. Kendra Greene

14. *Drown/Sever/Sing* by Lina Maria Ferreira Cabeza-Vanegas

15. *The All-New* by Ian Hatcher

16. *Book of Interludes* by Grace Shuyi Liew

17. *The Surrender* by Scott Esposito

18. *Body Split: When Tongue Was Muscle* by Sarah Tourjee / *I Wanted Just To Be Soft* by Temim Fruchter

"'I wear my body as infiltration' announces Grace Shuyi Liew, fusing erotics with geo-political, transborder resistance. The radical, unflinching 'I' of these poems shines 'like a sun that desiccates rather than animates,' searing the symbology of systemic horrors into a map of private, locatable griefs. The intelligence here is wickedly formidable, flexing and extinguishing itself, refusing to channel its own sense of embodied damage and colonization into narratives of redemption or rapture. These poems ask us 'To un-see, to pre-see, to march / latent cognition into / an unmarked grave.' I'm thrilled to relinquish my sight to these marvelous poems that speak from the place where 'the sky turned over and vanished us.'"

—**Lara Glenum**

"The poems in *Book of Interludes* discern the guts of a thing, the qualities of the body with "postcolonial tan lines." Grace Shuyi Liew grapples with the alienation of our physical postures throughout her lithe and rhetorically capacious lines. These poems say: "Nothing that comes out of / Me is an accident." These poems speak to the coherence of bodies that are flung onto a faulty framework and then requested to speak and be. Bodies matter, and so does every word, and so does the inescapable grid of power that permeates these ferociously smart and lyrically unflinching poems. "What you have stolen I don't even want anymore," they say. Instead, "Do you: Carry murder in yourself?"

—**Ginger Ko**, author of *Motherlover*